DISASTERS
BY THE
NUMBERS

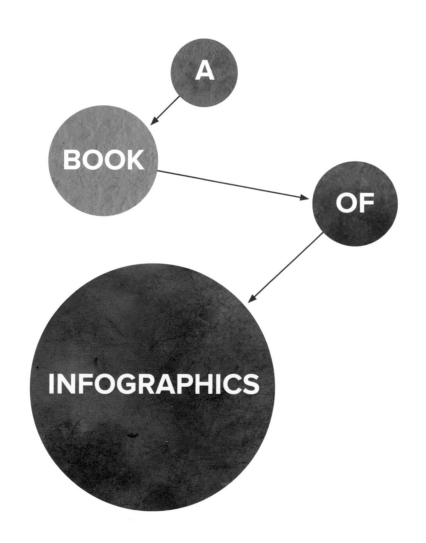

A

BOOK

OF

INFOGRAPHICS

STEVE JENKINS

HOUGHTON MIFFLIN HARCOURT · BOSTON · NEW YORK

Earth
Disasters caused by movements of the earth

Weather
Disasters caused by wind, water, and extremes of temperature

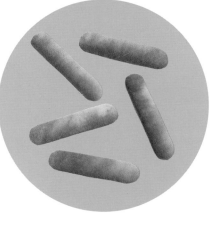

Life
Disasters caused by living things

Space
Out-of-this-world disasters

The earth is a restless planet. Continents collide in slow motion, causing earthquakes and volcanoes. Mountains rise and fall, and violent storms come and go. These things have been going on for billions of years. But when humans and their homes and towns and cities are affected by one of these events, the result is called a natural disaster. Some disasters, such as earthquakes, are sudden and unstoppable. Others, like droughts and sea level rise, happen in what seems to us like slow motion. Many of these events would happen whether people were here or not. Others are the result of something humans have done to the planet without understanding the consequences. Most natural disasters are local, affecting just one part of the earth. But a few threaten the entire planet and everyone living on it.

CONTENTS

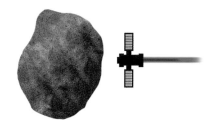

Natural disasters can be complicated

In this book, natural disasters are organized into four categories: **earth**, **weather**, **life**, and **space**. But many disasters have multiple effects. Some are immediate, while others are felt long after the original event. For example, a series of disastrous events often follows a large volcanic eruption.

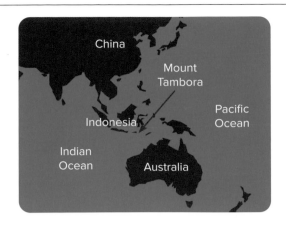

Tambora

In April of 1815, Mount Tambora, a volcano in Indonesia, exploded. It was the most powerful volcanic eruption of the past 10,000 years.

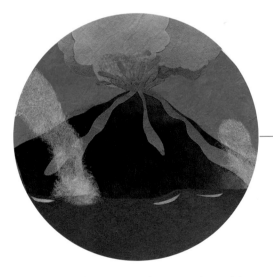

The force of the blast destroyed anything living within a few miles of the volcano.

Pyroclastic flow

Superheated ash and gas flowed down the volcano at more than 100 mph (160 kph).*

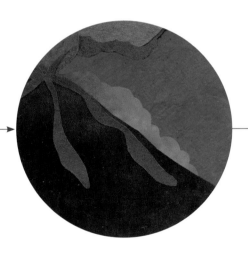

The pyroclastic flow killed anything left alive on the island. More than 10,000 people were killed almost instantly.

Tsunami

The shock of the eruption created a tsunami — a giant wave.

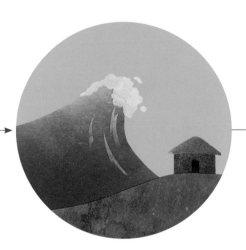

The surge of water washed away towns and villages on nearby islands.

Timeline of a large explosive eruption and its aftereffects

eruption begins   minutes   hours

*mph = miles per hour
kph = kilometers per hour

The eruption of Mount Tambora blew the top off the mountain. The explosion was heard by people more than 1,200 miles (1,931 kilometers) away, who thought they were hearing cannon fire.

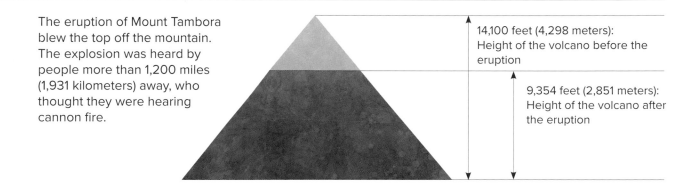

14,100 feet (4,298 meters): Height of the volcano before the eruption

9,354 feet (2,851 meters): Height of the volcano after the eruption

Ash fall

Ash and pumice — volcanic rock — rained down over a huge area. In some places it was many feet deep.

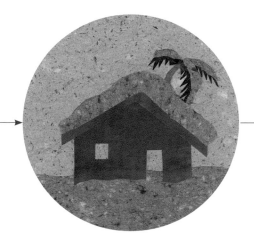

The weight of the ash collapsed houses and killed crops and livestock on the surrounding islands. As a result, 80,000 people perished of starvation and disease.

Atmospheric effects

Gases from the volcano were blasted high into the atmosphere. They mixed with water to form tiny droplets of sulphuric acid.*

High-altitude winds spread the droplets around the world. They reflected sunlight back into space and cooled the planet.

Global cooling

Many parts of the world were unusually cold in 1816 and 1817.

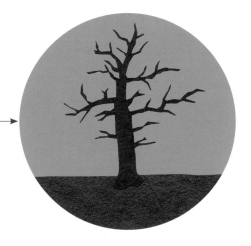

In some places, the cold weather caused crops to fail and livestock to perish. Over the next year or two, thousands of people around the world died of starvation.

hours to weeks

weeks to months

months to years

The definition of words in blue can be found in the glossary on pages 46–47.

The earth moves

Earth's crust is broken into more than a dozen pieces, called tectonic plates. The plates — and the continents on them — are in constant motion. On average, they move at about the same speed that your fingernails grow. Most earthquakes occur where two plates meet. As they slide past each other, the plates can get stuck, sometimes for centuries. Pressure builds up until the plates suddenly move, releasing energy and shaking the ground.

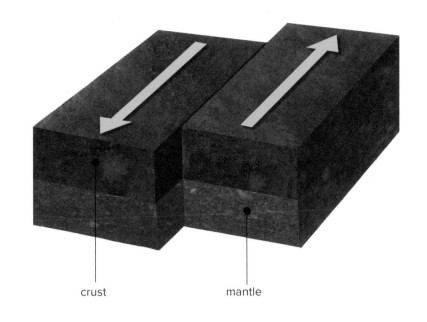

crust   mantle

Deadly earthquakes

There are hundreds of thousands of earthquakes every year. Most can only be detected by scientific instruments, but about 100 each year are strong enough to cause damage. The graph below highlights a few of the serious quakes of the past 500 years.

The size of the circles on the graph represents the number of fatalities caused by each earthquake.

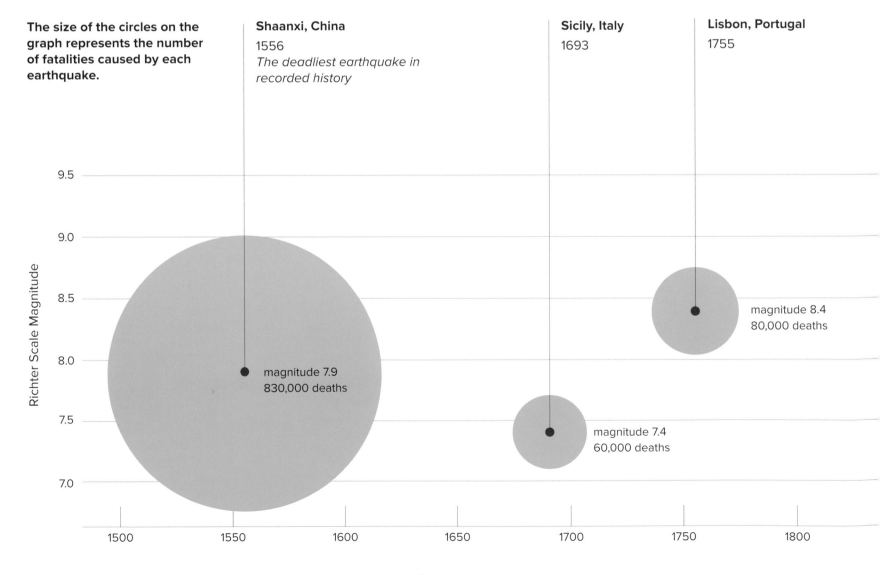

Shaanxi, China
1556
The deadliest earthquake in recorded history

magnitude 7.9
830,000 deaths

Sicily, Italy
1693

magnitude 7.4
60,000 deaths

Lisbon, Portugal
1755

magnitude 8.4
80,000 deaths

Richter Scale Magnitude

9.5
9.0
8.5
8.0
7.5
7.0

1500   1550   1600   1650   1700   1750   1800

Some of the things that make an earthquake deadly

Building collapse, falling masonry

Tsunami

Landslide or avalanche

Fire (caused by broken gas lines or overturned oil lamps)

Liquefaction — intense vibration makes wet soil act like a liquid

The Richter Scale

There are different ways of measuring the strength of an earthquake. One of the most commonly used is the Richter Scale, which ranks earthquakes on a 1–9 scale. Each step on the scale represents a 10X increase in magnitude (a magnitude 4 quake is ten times as powerful as a magnitude 3 quake).

1 Usually not felt.

2 Some people feel movement. Hanging fixtures sway slightly.

3 Most people notice. Objects indoors may shake or rattle.

4 Noticeable shaking. Objects may fall off shelves. Slight damage to structures.

5 Furniture may fall over. Major damage to poorly built structures.

6 Moderate to severe damage to most buildings. Difficult to remain standing.

7 Almost all structures damaged. Many buildings collapse. Impossible to remain standing.

8 Most buildings severely damaged or destroyed. People and objects thrown into the air.

9 The surface of the earth buckles. Total destruction of almost all buildings.

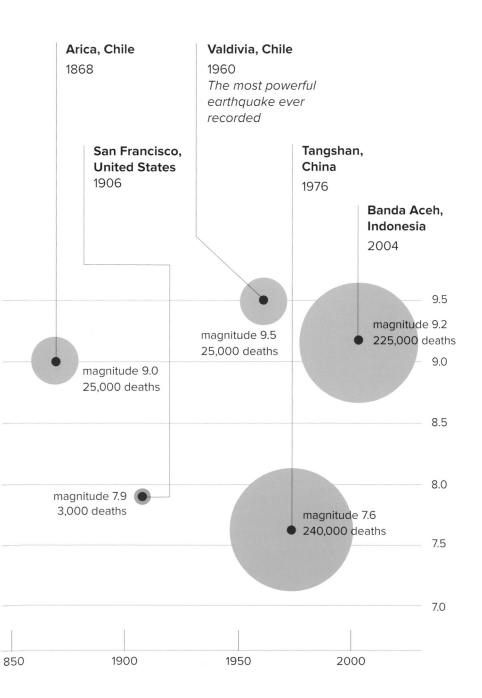

Arica, Chile
1868

Valdivia, Chile
1960
The most powerful earthquake ever recorded

San Francisco, United States
1906

Tangshan, China
1976

Banda Aceh, Indonesia
2004

magnitude 9.5
25,000 deaths

magnitude 9.2
225,000 deaths

magnitude 9.0
25,000 deaths

magnitude 7.9
3,000 deaths

magnitude 7.6
240,000 deaths

9.5
9.0
8.5
8.0
7.5
7.0

850   1900   1950   2000

Lava, ash, and fire

The crust of the earth is a layer of rock about as thick, compared to the earth as a whole, as an apple's skin is to an apple. The crust floats on the mantle, a much thicker layer of hot rock that contains pockets of molten rock, or magma. Sometimes magma reaches the surface and escapes in a volcanic eruption. Some of these eruptions are gentle. Others are powerfully explosive.

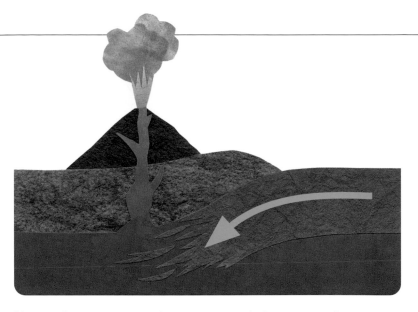

Many volcanoes occur where two crustal plates meet. One section of crust dives beneath another and is melted by the heat of the mantle. The molten rock, or magma, rises and bursts from the surface as a volcano.

Volcanic dangers

What makes a volcano deadly?

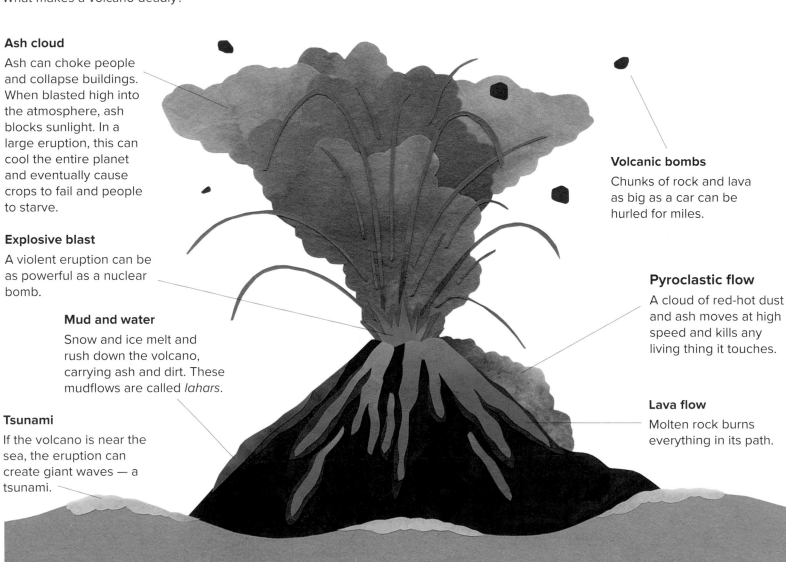

Ash cloud

Ash can choke people and collapse buildings. When blasted high into the atmosphere, ash blocks sunlight. In a large eruption, this can cool the entire planet and eventually cause crops to fail and people to starve.

Explosive blast

A violent eruption can be as powerful as a nuclear bomb.

Mud and water

Snow and ice melt and rush down the volcano, carrying ash and dirt. These mudflows are called *lahars*.

Tsunami

If the volcano is near the sea, the eruption can create giant waves — a tsunami.

Volcanic bombs

Chunks of rock and lava as big as a car can be hurled for miles.

Pyroclastic flow

A cloud of red-hot dust and ash moves at high speed and kills any living thing it touches.

Lava flow

Molten rock burns everything in its path.

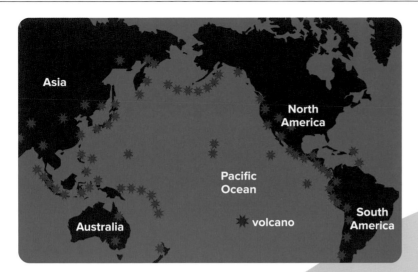

Asia

North America

Pacific Ocean

Australia

South America

✳ volcano

Three-quarters of Earth's volcanoes are found on the **Ring of Fire**, a chain of volcanoes around the Pacific Ocean. They occur where the Pacific Plate collides with other tectonic plates.

VEI 5
Mount St. Helens
Washington,
United States, 1980
57 deaths

VEI 6
Santa María
Guatemala, 1902
5,000 deaths

VEI 6
Novarupta
Alaska,
United States, 1912
no deaths
(The eruption
occurred in an
uninhabited area.)

VEI 6
Krakatoa
Indonesia, 1883
36,000 deaths

The VEI

Volcanoes are rated from 1 to 8 on the VEI (Volcanic Explosivity Index). This scale is based on the force of the eruption and on the amount of lava, ash, and rock ejected.

An eruption that can cause serious local damage occurs somewhere on Earth about once every 10 years. Eruptions that seriously affect the entire planet are much rarer, taking place about once every 10,000 years.

VEI 7
Tambora
Indonesia, 1815
90,000 deaths

This is the largest eruption of the past 10,000 years, and the eruption with the greatest human death toll.

VEI 8
Toba
Sumatra
75,000 years ago
deaths unknown

This is the largest eruption of the past 25 million years. It ejected enough ash, rocks, and lava to cover a thousand football fields to a depth of two miles (3.2 kilometers).

VEI 8
Taupō
New Zealand
26,000 years ago
deaths unknown

The size of the circles represents the amount of material ejected in an eruption.

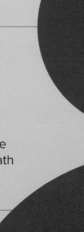

Get to high ground!

In the open ocean, a tsunami — an unusually large wave or set of waves — travels at speeds of up to 500 mph (805 kph). But when the tsunami waves reach shallow water, they slow down and grow taller, sometimes reaching heights of 100 feet (30 meters) or more. Depending upon where the tsunami originated, people in low-lying coastal areas have anywhere from a few minutes to a few hours to get away from the coast or climb to safety.

The largest tsunami ever witnessed occurred in Alaska in 1958. An earthquake dropped millions of tons of rock into Lituya Bay. The resulting wave was 1,720 feet (524 meters) high.

The deadliest tsunami in history occurred in Indonesia in 2004. An undersea earthquake created waves that killed more than 225,000 people.

Most tsunamis are caused by earthquakes

Timeline of a large tsunami

time elapsed: seconds

5 minutes

A powerful quake takes place beneath the seafloor.

The spreading water forms a series of fast-moving waves. In deep water, they are only a foot or two high and often go unnoticed.

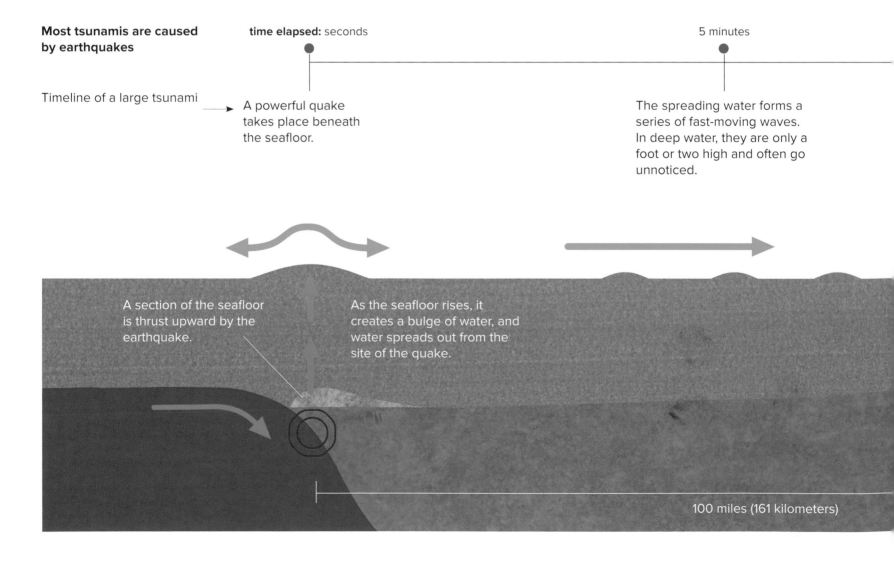

A section of the seafloor is thrust upward by the earthquake.

As the seafloor rises, it creates a bulge of water, and water spreads out from the site of the quake.

100 miles (161 kilometers)

Tsunamis can also be caused by

Explosive **volcanic eruptions**

Landslides, which are sometimes the result of an erupting volcano or an earthquake. An underwater landslide can also create a tsunami.

Meteorites and **asteroids** hitting the water. These events are rare, but can be devastating.

Large chunks of **ice** breaking off a glacier and falling into the sea

12 minutes

As the waves reach shallower water, they begin to slow and build in height.

15 minutes

Eventually, the waves break and wash over low-lying coasts. In some tsunamis, waves a few minutes apart can continue to arrive for hours.

Sometimes tsunami waves don't curl and break, but act more like a fast-moving high tide. This is why tsunamis are sometimes called "tidal waves," even though they don't have any connection to the tides (which are caused by the gravitational pull of the Moon and Sun).

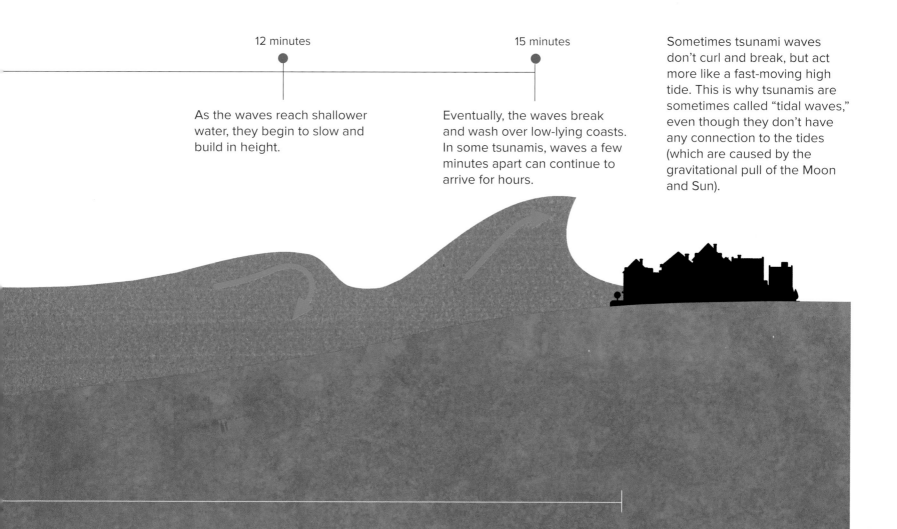

Dirt, rocks, and mud

Mountains are constantly being eroded — worn down by wind and rain. This is usually a gradual process that happens over millions of years. But sometimes mountainsides come crashing down in the blink of an eye.

In 2010, heavy rains fell on Gansu, China. In some areas, it rained four inches (10 centimeters) in one hour. A wall of rocks and mud five stories high swept down a river and through several towns, killing more than 1,700 people.

What causes landslides and mudslides?

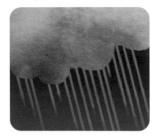

Heavy rainfall softens and weakens the soil that holds hillsides in place.

One of the effects of a **volcanic eruption** can be a lahar — a surge of mud and ash carried by melted snow and ice.

When an **earthquake** shakes the ground, it can cause unstable rocks and soil on steep mountainsides to tumble downhill.

When a **wildfire** destroys the vegetation that helps hold a hillside in place, even a light rain can cause mud and rocks to tumble downhill.

Snow and ice

Snow can accumulate on steep mountain slopes until something disturbs it. When that happens, a mass of snow and ice can break loose and slide downhill at speeds of more than 200 mph (322 kph). It's an avalanche, and it can snap big trees like matchsticks and bury a skier — or a whole town.

Most avalanches are caused by people — skiers, hikers, or snowmobilers. Slides typically happen on slopes between 30 and 50 degrees.

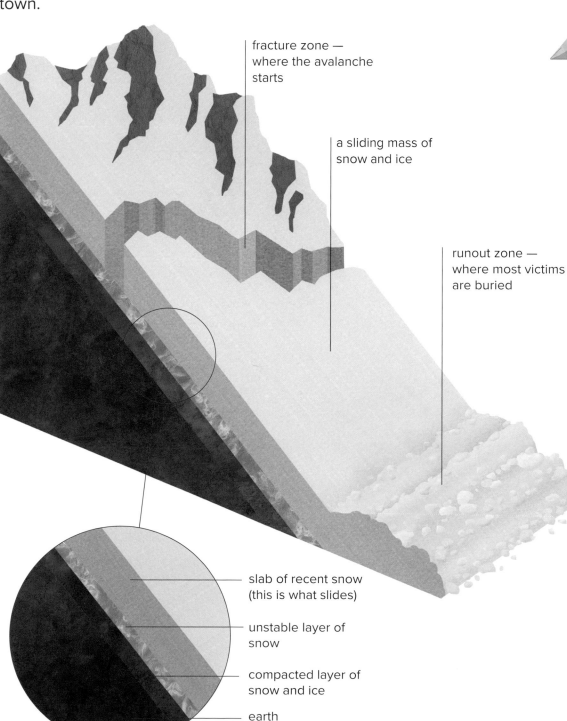

fracture zone — where the avalanche starts

a sliding mass of snow and ice

runout zone — where most victims are buried

slab of recent snow (this is what slides)

unstable layer of snow

compacted layer of snow and ice

earth

The deadliest avalanche

In 1970, a magnitude 7.9 earthquake struck off the coast of Peru. The quake shook loose the deadliest avalanche ever recorded. More than 20,000 people were killed.

A single snowflake is delicate and almost weightless. But when enough snowflakes pile up and start to slide, the results can be disastrous.

Rare but deadly

Some of the threats we face are serious, but unlikely to affect us. That's because they don't happen very often, or they take place only in unusual situations.

Yellowstone supervolcano

Supervolcanoes are powerful but infrequent, occurring about once every 100,000 years. The eruption of the supervolcano beneath Yellowstone National Park buried much of the United States in ash and caused the entire planet to cool down for years. Someday, the supervolcano will go off again. But scientists assure us that there will be warning signs before that happens.

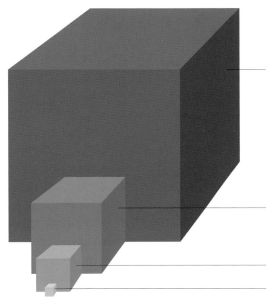

The amount of ash, rock, and lava ejected

Yellowstone supervolcano

2,000,000 years ago

It ejected enough ash, rock, and lava to fill a cube more than eight miles (13 kilometers) on each side.

Tambora, 1815 (the largest eruption of the past 10,000 years)

Krakatoa, 1883

Mount St. Helens, 1980

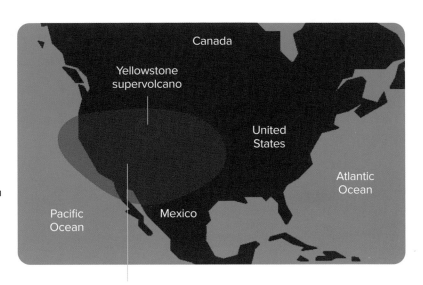

Area covered by ash in the Yellowstone eruption two million years ago

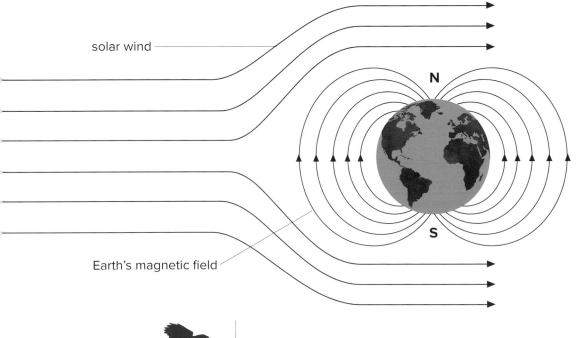

solar wind

Earth's magnetic field

Magnetic flip

Earth has a magnetic field and magnetic poles. The magnetic field helps protect life on Earth by deflecting harmful cosmic rays coming from the Sun. Because of changes in Earth's core, the magnetic poles sometimes flip (a compass would point south instead of north). This last happened 780,000 years ago, and it will happen again. The reversed magnetic field will be weaker than the one we have now, and it will allow dangerous solar radiation — known as *solar wind* — to reach Earth's surface.

Many animals use Earth's magnetic field to guide them as they migrate. A reversed or weakened magnetic field could be a serious problem for them.

Canary Islands megatsunami

A volcano in the Canary Islands poses one of the planet's greatest geological threats. An eruption there could send a large chunk of the island plummeting into the Atlantic Ocean, creating a megatsunami — a series of enormous waves — as high as 3,000 feet (914 meters). Hours later, the waves would reach the eastern coast of the Americas. They could still be more than 100 feet (30 meters) high, and they would wash away many coastal towns and cites.

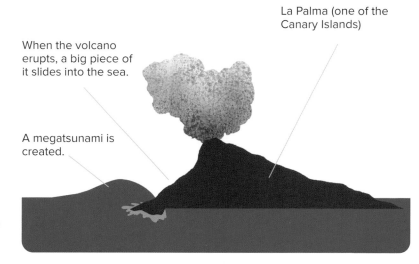

When the volcano erupts, a big piece of it slides into the sea.

La Palma (one of the Canary Islands)

A megatsunami is created.

Estimated height of the megatsunami when it reaches North America

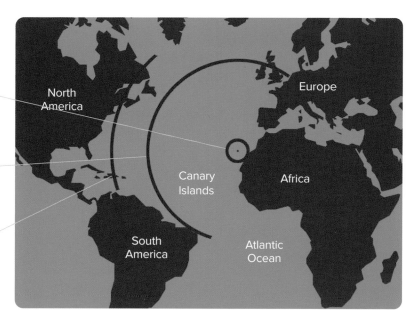

megatsunami one hour after the eruption

megatsunami six hours hour after the eruption

megatsunami eight hours hour after the eruption

North America

Europe

Canary Islands

Africa

South America

Atlantic Ocean

Lethal lake

Lake Nyos, in the African nation of Cameroon, lies in a volcanically active area. In 1986, the lake water was saturated with carbon dioxide gas. This gas is not poisonous, but it can kill by suffocation. Something, perhaps a small earthquake, caused the CO_2 to bubble out of the lake water. Being heavier than air, the gas flowed into a nearby valley. More than 1,700 people, as well as all the animals in the area — even insects — died.

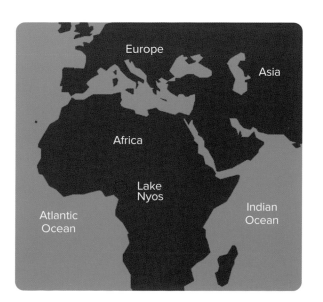

Europe

Asia

Africa

Lake Nyos

Atlantic Ocean

Indian Ocean

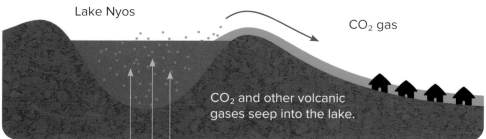

Lake Nyos

CO_2 gas

CO_2 and other volcanic gases seep into the lake.

Killer storms

In different parts of the world, intense tropical storms are called hurricanes, typhoons, or cyclones. They are the most powerful storms on Earth, and they can last for days, with destructive winds, deadly storm surge, and heavy rainfall.

How storms are named

Every tropical storm is given a name, alternating between male and female names. Different parts of the world use different lists of names. For storms in the Atlantic, the names begin with the letter *A* and proceed in alphabetical order. The names for 2022 begin with Alex, Bonnie, Colin, and Danielle.

If there are more than twenty-one named storms in the Atlantic (the letters *Q, U, X, Y,* and *Z* are not used), there is a second set of male and female names that will be used.

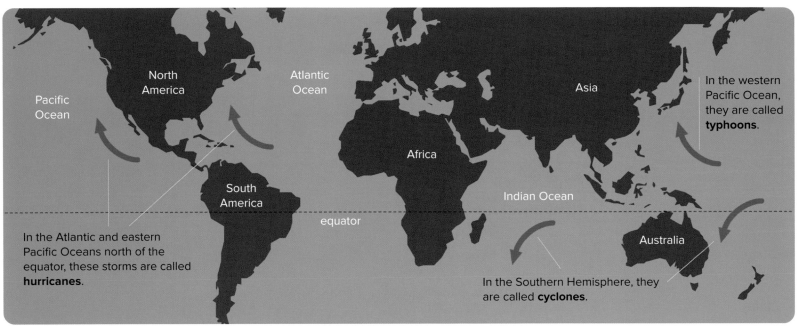

In the western Pacific Ocean, they are called **typhoons**.

In the Atlantic and eastern Pacific Oceans north of the equator, these storms are called **hurricanes**.

In the Southern Hemisphere, they are called **cyclones**.

Anatomy of a hurricane

average width of storm = 300 miles (483 kilometers)

average width of eye = 30 miles (48 kilometers)

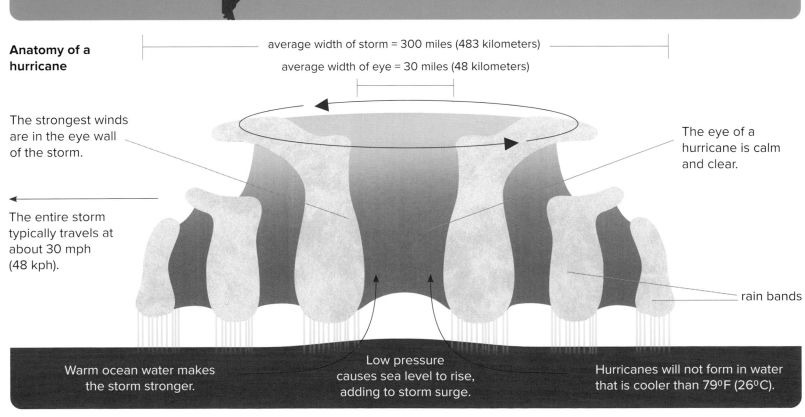

The strongest winds are in the eye wall of the storm.

The eye of a hurricane is calm and clear.

The entire storm typically travels at about 30 mph (48 kph).

rain bands

Warm ocean water makes the storm stronger.

Low pressure causes sea level to rise, adding to storm surge.

Hurricanes will not form in water that is cooler than 79°F (26°C).

Due to the rotation of the earth, tropical storms rotate counterclockwise in the Northern Hemisphere . . .

. . . and clockwise in the Southern Hemisphere.

Record wind speeds

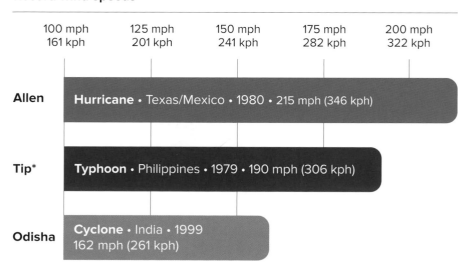

	100 mph 161 kph	125 mph 201 kph	150 mph 241 kph	175 mph 282 kph	200 mph 322 kph

Allen — Hurricane · Texas/Mexico · 1980 · 215 mph (346 kph)

Tip* — Typhoon · Philippines · 1979 · 190 mph (306 kph)

Odisha — Cyclone · India · 1999 162 mph (261 kph)

* 1,380 miles (2,221 km) in diameter — largest tropical storm ever measured

The hurricane intensity scale is based on wind speed

Category 1
75–95 mph (121–153 kph) winds

Some broken tree branches, damage to house roofs and powerlines.

Category 2
96–110 mph (154–177 kph) winds

Some trees uprooted. Serious damage to homes and other structures. Some roofs blown off.

Category 3
111–129 mph (178–208 kph) winds

Extensive damage to homes and commercial buildings. Many trees toppled. Loss of electricity and running water for days or weeks.

Category 4
130–156 mph (209–251 kph) winds

Catastrophic damage to houses and other structures. Many destroyed. Roads impassable due to flooding and downed trees. Power and water supply lost for weeks or months.

Category 5
higher than 157 mph (252 kph) winds

Almost complete destruction of houses and buildings. Deadly storm surge. Area left uninhabitable for weeks or months.

Twister!

A tornado forms when some of the energy in a thunderstorm is converted into a spinning column of air that reaches from the clouds to the ground. Tornadoes are much smaller than hurricanes, but wind speeds in a tornado can be higher. Tornadoes can cause massive damage to buildings, vehicles, livestock, and people.

Tornadoes occur in many parts of the world.

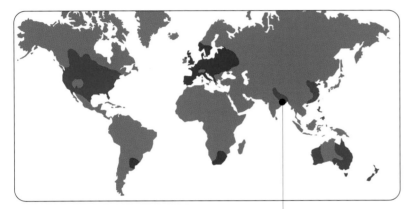

But more than four out of five of the world's tornadoes occur in the United States.

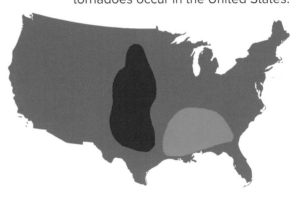

Where tornadoes happen

In 1989, the deadliest tornado in history killed 1,300 people in Bangladesh.

Two areas in the American Midwest and South are known for frequent and violent tornadoes.

 Tornado Alley

Dixie Alley

Taking a tornado ride

People caught in a tornado may be killed or injured by flying debris or by being dropped from a great height. But a few people have been sucked into the air, spun around, and set back down without much damage. These three lucky people (and one pony) survived their encounter with a tornado with only minor scrapes.

Tennessee, 2008

An eleven-month-old baby was torn from his mother's arms, lifted into the air, and set down 300 feet (91 meters) away.

South Dakota, 1955

A nine-year-old girl and her pony were picked up and carried 1,000 feet (305 meters).

Missouri, 2006

A nineteen-year-old man was sucked out of a trailer and carried 1,307 feet (398 meters).

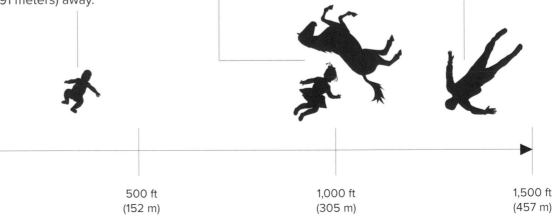

| 0 ft (0 m) | 500 ft (152 m) | 1,000 ft (305 m) | 1,500 ft (457 m) |

The tornado rating scale

Tornadoes are rated on a five-step scale called the EF Scale. It is based on maximum wind speeds and the amount of damage done by a tornado on the ground.

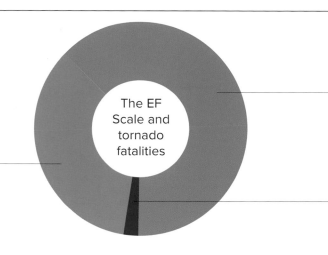

The EF Scale and tornado fatalities

Sixty-five percent of tornadoes are rated **EF-0** or **EF-1**. These twisters cause few deaths.

Thirty-three percent of tornadoes are rated **EF-2** or **EF-3**. They cause 30 percent of tornado-related deaths.

Only two percent of tornadoes are rated **EF-4** or **EF-5**, but they cause 70 percent of tornado-related deaths.

Weak: EF-0 and EF-1

65–110 mph
(105–177 kph) winds

Slight to moderate damage to trees and buildings

Strong: EF-2 and EF-3

111–165 mph
(179–266 kph) winds

Serious damage to trees and buildings
Extensive power outages

Devastating: EF-4 and EF-5

166–over 200 mph
(267–over 322 kph) winds

Total destruction of most structures
Cars and trucks flipped and blown away

Tornado records

The Tri-State Tornado of 1925 holds multiple tornado records. It stayed on the ground for 3½ hours (most tornadoes last for just a few minutes). Its path was 219 miles (352 kilometers) long, a world record. It also holds the record for fastest-moving tornado — at one point, it was clocked at 73 mph (117 kph). It killed 695 people — making it the second most deadly tornado in history.

The El Reno, Oklahoma, EF-3 tornado of 2013 was the widest tornado ever measured.

Typical tornado 1,200 feet (366 meters) wide

El Reno tornado 2.6 miles (4,184 meters) wide

Empire State Building (for size comparison)

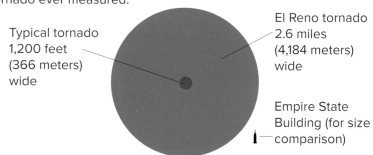

Path of the Tri-State Tornado through the American Midwest

The highest wind speed ever observed on Earth was in the Bridge Creek–Moore EF-5 tornado of 1999 in Oklahoma.

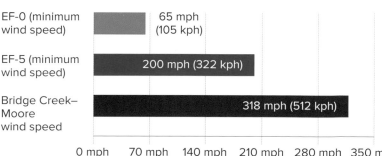

EF-0 (minimum wind speed) — 65 mph (105 kph)

EF-5 (minimum wind speed) — 200 mph (322 kph)

Bridge Creek–Moore wind speed — 318 mph (512 kph)

| 0 mph (0 kph) | 70 mph (113 kph) | 140 mph (225 kph) | 210 mph (338 kph) | 280 mph (451 kph) | 350 mph (563 kph) |

Rising water

In some floods, the water is calm and rises slowly. But in a *flash flood,* a turbulent, fast-moving wall of water arrives without warning. Floods may be the result of heavy rains, storm-driven surges, or the collapse of natural or man-made dams.

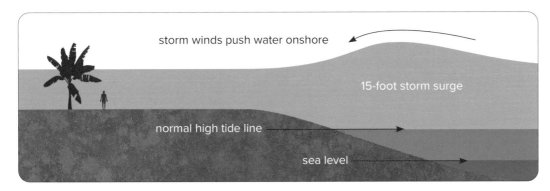

storm winds push water onshore

15-foot storm surge

normal high tide line

sea level

Storm surge

In 1900, a hurricane came ashore at Galveston, Texas. It brought a 15-foot (4½-meter) storm surge and caused 8,000 deaths, most of them by drowning.

Quake, slide, flood

In 1841, in what is now Pakistan, (**1**) an earthquake triggered a landslide that blocked the Indus River for months. (**2**) A 500-foot-deep (152-meter-deep) lake formed. (**3**) When the natural rock dam failed, it released what was probably the largest flood in recorded history. No one knows how many people were killed, but it must have been many thousands.

Dam failure

The dam above Johnstown, Pennsylvania, was man-made. But days of heavy rain caused it to collapse in 1889. It was the deadliest flash flood in US history. More than 2,200 people were killed when a 40-foot (12-meter) wall of water swept through the town.

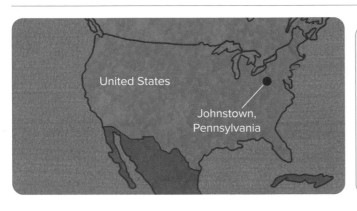

United States

Johnstown, Pennsylvania

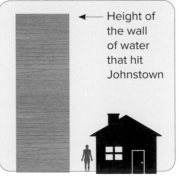

Height of the wall of water that hit Johnstown

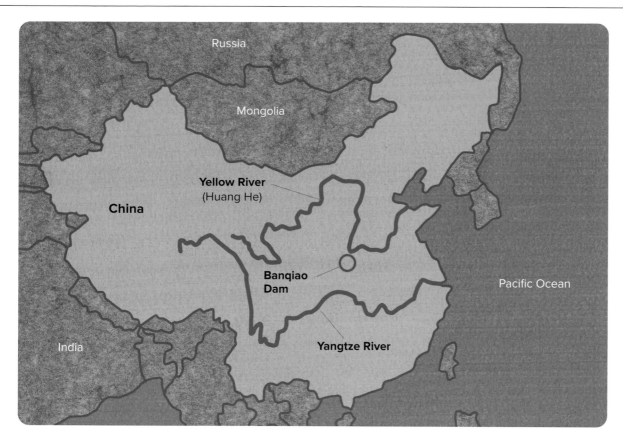

The China floods

China has experienced more deadly floods than any other country. The Yangtze River — the third-longest river in the world — has repeatedly overflowed its banks. The Yellow River, or Huang He, has also flooded many times. These rivers run through low, fertile lands that are home to millions of people.

1887

Yellow River flood

After heavy rains, the river overflowed a system of dikes.

900,000 fatalities

1931

Yangtze River floods

One of the worst natural disasters of all time. The flooding, due to heavy rains, lasted for several months.

2,000,000 fatalities

1935

Yangtze River flood

Caused by unusually heavy rainfall

145,000 fatalities

1938

Yellow River flood

China was at war. Dikes were intentionally breached to slow the Japanese army.

500,000 fatalities

1975

Banqiao Dam

This dam, on the Ru River in central China, failed after intense rains.

230,000 fatalities

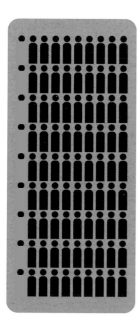
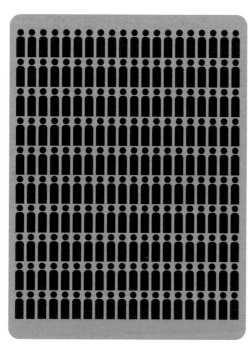

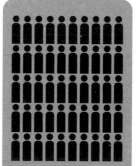
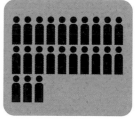

Each figure represents 10,000 deaths.

Wind, rain, lightning, hail

Severe thunderstorms can be deadly. The heavy rain that often accompanies a storm can cause flash floods. Wind and hail can damage property and sometimes injure or even kill people. Tornadoes get their start in thunderstorms. And lightning kills thousands of people a year.

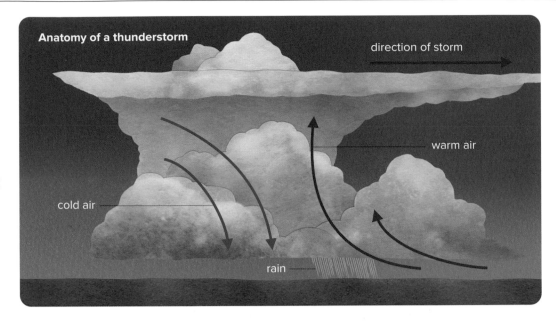

Anatomy of a thunderstorm

direction of storm

warm air

cold air

rain

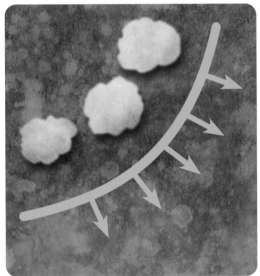

Thunderstorms often take on the shape of an anvil. The technical name of a thunderstorm cloud is *cumulonimbus,* but it is often called an anvil cloud. ▶

◀ Sometimes a line of thunderstorms creates a band of hurricane-force winds that can be hundreds of miles wide. This dangerous phenomenon is called a *derecho* (*de-**ray**-cho*).

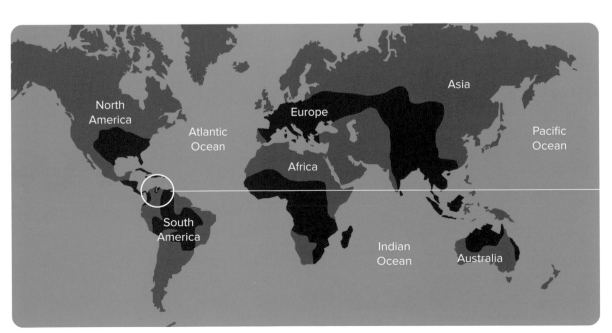

North America

Atlantic Ocean

Europe

Asia

Africa

Pacific Ocean

South America

Indian Ocean

Australia

Thunderstorm hot spots
The areas in red experience at least 20 thunderstorms a year. At any given time, there are about 2,000 thunderstorms happening around the world.

The top thunderstorm and lightning spot in the world is a lake in Venezuela, where there is, on average, a thunderstorm 300 days a year.

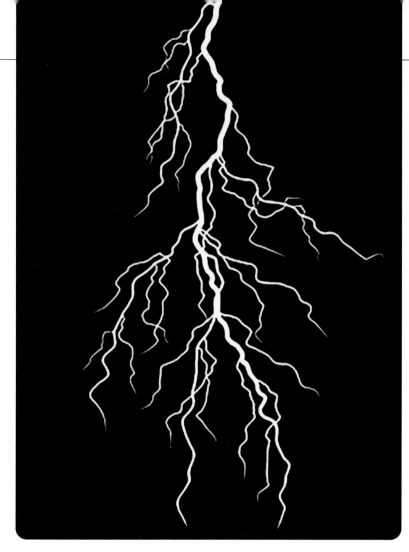

Shocking

Lightning always accompanies a thunderstorm, and is the cause of many deaths, injuries, and forest fires.

Lightning casualties

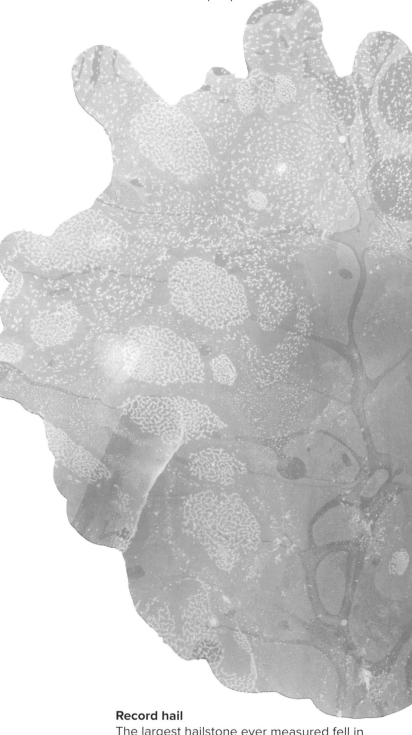

Each symbol represents 6,000 people. About 240,000 people a year are struck by lightning around the world. Serious injury results for about 180,000 of these victims. As many as 24,000 are killed.

- struck but not seriously injured
- seriously injured but not killed
- killed

Ice from the sky

Hail — solid balls of ice that can be as small as a blueberry or as large as a cantaloupe — sometimes falls during a thunderstorm. Large hail can damage cars, buildings, trees, and crops. It can even be deadly. A hailstorm in India in 1888 killed more than 230 people.

Record hail

The largest hailstone ever measured fell in South Dakota in 2010. It was eight inches (20 centimeters) in diameter. (Shown here at actual size)

Snow and wind

There are snowstorms, and then there are blizzards. A blizzard can bring a large area — even a big city — to a standstill. A blizzard's cold, wind, and snow combine to create potentially deadly conditions.

In January of 1888, a sudden drop in temperature and heavy, drifting snow caught people — and trains — unaware. The storm was called the Schoolhouse Blizzard, and it killed 235 people in the American Midwest.

What is a blizzard?

A snowstorm has to meet three requirements to be considered a blizzard:

❶ Wind

In a blizzard, the wind blows at least 35 mph (56 kph). In a severe blizzard, the wind blows at more than 45 mph (72 kph).

❷ Visibility

Blowing snow reduces visibility — the distance one can see before everything disappears in the snow — to less than ¼ mile (402 meters).

❸ Duration

The snowy, windy conditions must last for at least three hours.

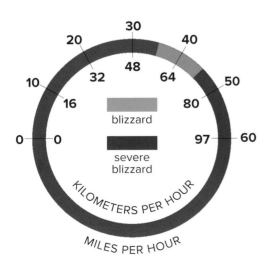

blizzard

severe blizzard

KILOMETERS PER HOUR

MILES PER HOUR

As objects in a blizzard get farther away, they begin to disappear into the snow.

| 100 feet (30 meters) away | 400 feet (122 meters) away | 800 feet (244 meters) away | 1,200 feet (366 meters) away |

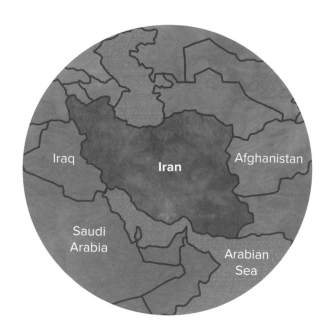

A deadly blizzard

Twenty-six feet (8 meters) of snow fell in Iran in a 1972 blizzard. Hundreds of villages were completely buried, and 4,000 people died.

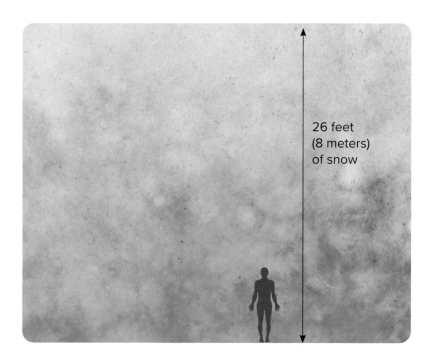

26 feet (8 meters) of snow

The Great Blizzard of 1888

Fifty inches (1¼ meters) of snow fell on parts of New England. High winds created snowdrifts that were 50 feet (15 meters) deep in places, and 400 people died in the storm.

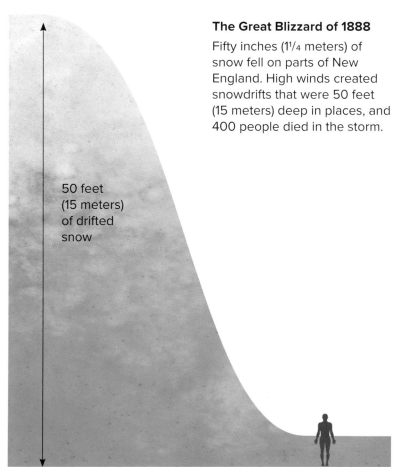

50 feet (15 meters) of drifted snow

What do volcanoes have to do with blizzards?

In 1883, the South Pacific island of Krakatoa exploded. It was one of the most powerful volcanic eruptions in recorded history. The ash and gases blasted into the atmosphere reflected sunlight and cooled the planet for several years. Scientists think that the eruption may have helped cause the intense blizzards of 1885–1888 in the United States.

Waiting for rain

A drought is a period of months or years in which there is less rainfall or snowfall than usual. This reduces moisture in the soil, lowers groundwater levels, and dries up lakes and streams. Aside from pandemics, droughts have been responsible for more human deaths than any other kind of natural disaster.

Ancient droughts

By looking at the growth rings in old trees and the sediments from long-ago lakes and rivers, scientists can tell when and where severe droughts occurred.

A moving wall of dirt

During a drought, the soil dries out and can be picked up and carried by the wind. It's a dust storm, and it can smother fields and fill houses with dirt. The midwestern United States endured repeated dust storms during the Dust Bowl of the 1930s.

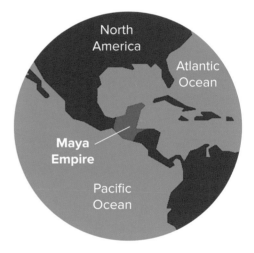

Out of Africa

Between 90,000 and 130,000 years ago, parts of Africa experienced a series of severe droughts. Lakes and rivers dried up, and forests turned to deserts. These changes may have given early humans a reason to leave Africa and spread into other parts of the world.

Egypt's Old Kingdom

Ancient Egypt was home to one of the most advanced civilizations in the world. But by 4,000 years ago, Egypt's Old Kingdom was in decline. There is evidence of a drought at the same time, which many historians believe led to the end of Egypt as a world power.

The Maya Empire

For hundreds of years, the Mayans of Central America built impressive temples and practiced advanced mathematics and astronomy. But about 1,200 years ago, the Maya Empire collapsed. One of the main reasons for their downfall might have been a series of droughts that lasted for decades.

Drought: cause and effects

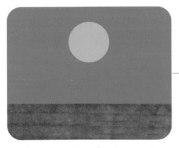

low levels of rain- and snowfall

soil dries out

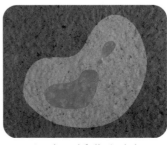

water level falls in lakes and rivers

groundwater is depleted

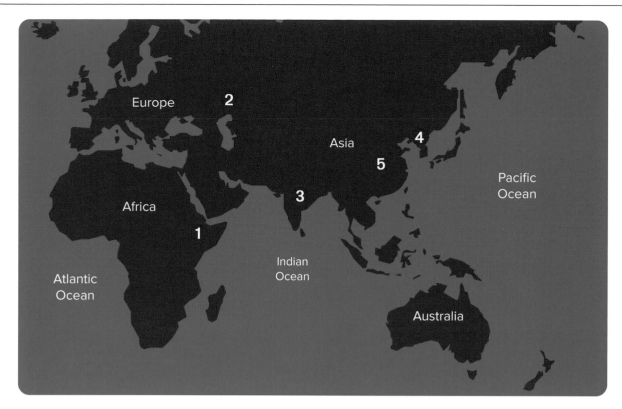

Drought and famine

Starvation is the most common cause of human death in a drought. When many people die from lack of food, it's called a *famine*. People weakened by lack of food are also more likely to die from disease. And droughts have led to war as people battled over limited supplies of water.

The map shows where some of the world's deadliest droughts have occurred.

❶ Ethiopian famine
1984–1985

The effects of a drought were made worse by war, which prevented aid from reaching starving people. More than one million people perished.

❷ Russian famine
1921–1922

Once again, crop failures caused by a drought were intensified by conflict and a political crisis. There were five million deaths.

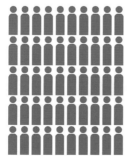

❸ Southern India famine
1876–1878

A widespread, severe drought affected much of Asia. In India, five and a half million people starved to death.

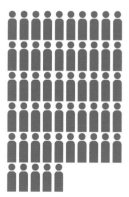

❹ North Korean famine
1994–1998

A drought — combined with the government's destructive policies — cost as many as two million lives.

❺ North China famine
1876–1879

The worst drought in China's history killed an estimated eleven million people.

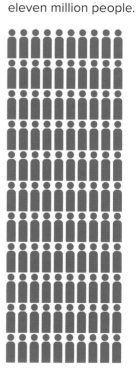

Each figure represents 100,000 human deaths.

Climate change and drought

The world is getting warmer at a rapid rate. As the climate warms, some parts of the world will get more rain and snow. But other parts will get much less. Higher temperatures are also drying out the soil more quickly.

(See pages 42–45 for more information about climate change.)

Too hot!

Extreme heat and drought often go together. But droughts happen over months or years. Heat waves are spikes in the temperature that last for days or weeks. Heat waves can be deadly, especially for older people or people in poor health who don't have air conditioning. The world is experiencing hotter and more frequent heat waves as the planet gets warmer.

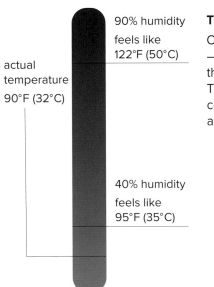

90% humidity feels like 122°F (50°C)

actual temperature 90°F (32°C)

40% humidity feels like 95°F (35°C)

The heat index

On hot days, high humidity — the amount of moisture in the air — makes it feel hotter. The *heat index* shows what a combination of temperature and humidity feels like.

What makes a heat wave deadly?

When it's very hot and there's no way to cool off, people are at risk for heatstroke. Normal body temperature is 98.6°F (37°C). But someone suffering from heatstroke will have a temperature of 104°F (40°C) or higher. Here are some of the other symptoms:

- Confusion
- Headache
- Nausea and vomiting
- Hot, dry skin. People with heatstroke don't sweat, even though their body is overheated.
- Rapid heart rate

Heatstroke is a serious medical condition. The best way to treat it is by cooling off the person with an ice bath, cold water, or wet towels.

Some serious heat

A heat wave is five or more days in a row when the temperature is more than 9°F (5°C) warmer than the average high temperature.

Each figure represents 500 deaths from heat.

maximum temperature reached during a heat wave

Pakistan, 2015
Temperatures reached 120°F (49°C). Two thousand people died as a result of the heat.

Eastern United States, 1901
It reached 108°F (42¼°C). Six weeks of record-breaking heat left 9,500 dead.

Greece, 1967
One thousand people were killed by temperatures reaching 107°F (41½°C).

Chicago, United States, 1995
More than 700 people died as the temperature climbed to 106°F (41°C).

France, 2003
More than 14,000 people were killed by a heat wave in Europe that reached 104°F (40°C). Thousands more died in other European countries.

Argentina, 1900
Unusually high humidity and 99°F (37°C) temperatures left more than 400 people dead.

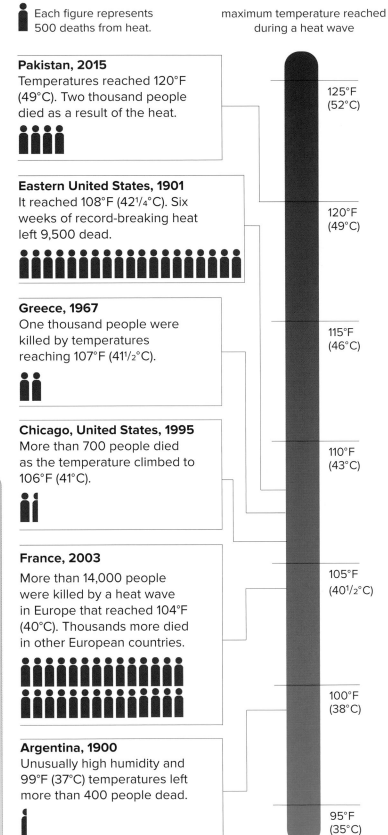

125°F (52°C)

120°F (49°C)

115°F (46°C)

110°F (43°C)

105°F (40½°C)

100°F (38°C)

95°F (35°C)

Too cold!

A cold wave, also called a cold snap, happens when the temperature drops far below normal lows in a short period of time. Cold waves can be dangerous to humans and animals. They can freeze water supplies and cause power failures, which leaves many people without heat.

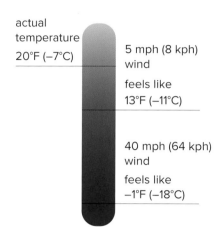

actual temperature
20°F (–7°C)

5 mph (8 kph) wind
feels like
13°F (–11°C)

40 mph (64 kph) wind
feels like
–1°F (–18°C)

Wind chill

On cold days, the wind makes it feel colder by drawing away the body's heat. A measurement of this effect is called the *wind chill factor*. Wind chill only applies when the temperature is below 50°F (10°C).

What makes a cold wave dangerous?

The most serious danger to people in cold weather is hypothermia, when the body temperature falls below 95°F (35°C). It's critical to get help for someone with hypothermia or they can die. Here are some of the symptoms:

- Shivering
- Slurred speech
- Sleepiness
- Disorientation
- Fast heart rate

When someone has hypothermia, it's important to get medical help quickly. If that's not possible, the person should be warmed with dry clothing and blankets. Someone who is not cold can help by wrapping themselves up in a blanket along with the person experiencing hypothermia.

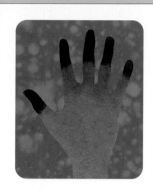

Frostbite — when exposed skin freezes and dies — is another risk of cold weather.

Some record cold temperatures around the world

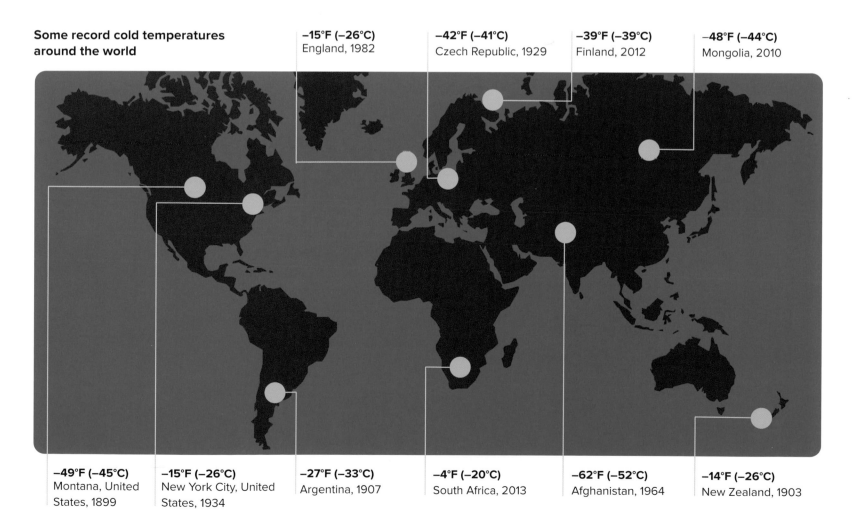

–15°F (–26°C)
England, 1982

–42°F (–41°C)
Czech Republic, 1929

–39°F (–39°C)
Finland, 2012

–48°F (–44°C)
Mongolia, 2010

–49°F (–45°C)
Montana, United States, 1899

–15°F (–26°C)
New York City, United States, 1934

–27°F (–33°C)
Argentina, 1907

–4°F (–20°C)
South Africa, 2013

–62°F (–52°C)
Afghanistan, 1964

–14°F (–26°C)
New Zealand, 1903

Increasing risk

As the climate warms, forests and grasslands dry out more quickly. This makes them vulnerable to wildfires. Sometimes the fires are started by a careless human tossing a cigarette into the grass. Other fires are started by downed power lines or lightning. However they begin, wildfires are one of nature's most terrifying spectacles. And once they start, they can spread quickly and burn forests, fields, and houses.

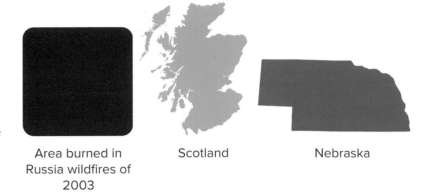

Area burned in Russia wildfires of 2003

Scotland

Nebraska

The area burned by a few historical wildfires

Russia: wildfires 2003
burned 77,000 square miles (200,000 square kilometers)

An area about the size of Scotland or the state of Nebraska. These were the largest wildfires ever recorded.

fatalities unknown

Australia: Black Summer 2019–2020
burned 73,000 square miles (189,000 square kilometers)

450 deaths

China: Black Dragon Fire 1987
burned 28,000 square miles (73,000 square kilometers)

200 deaths

Canada: Manitoba fires 1989
burned 12,664 square miles (33,000 square kilometers)

no reported fatalities

United States: West Coast fires 2020
burned 9,188 square miles (24,000 square kilometers) in California, Oregon, and Washington

40 deaths

Michigan: Peshtigo Fire 1871
burned 1,875 square miles (4,600 square kilometers)

1,200 to 2,500 deaths — the most caused by any wildfire in America

Fighting fires

Earthquakes, tornadoes, and many other natural disasters happen without warning, and there's nothing we can do to stop them. But we can — and do — fight wildfires. This airplane is dropping fire retardant to slow the spread of a fire.

Smoke

The smoke from a wildfire can spread over a large area and affect people thousands of miles away. Fine particles of smoke can damage people's lungs. This smoke is especially dangerous for small children and people with breathing problems.

Firestorms

If a fire gets large enough, it creates its own weather. Hot, rising air sucks wind into the center of the fire. It rises high into the atmosphere, where it forms a storm cloud (called a *pyrocumulus*). This cloud may generate lightning that strikes many miles away, starting new fires.

Fire tornado

Rarely, the updraft from a fire begins to rotate and creates a fiery tornado. Smaller versions of these spinning columns of fire are called fire whirls.

A whirring, flying plague

A grasshopper isn't what normally comes to mind when we think of a natural disaster. But given the right conditions, a normally harmless grasshopper population transforms into an unstoppable horde of locusts. Billions or trillions of these insects darken the sky as they swarm across the land, devouring every plant in their path.

Locusts swarming in East Africa

What makes a locust swarm deadly?

The insects are not poisonous and don't carry diseases. They don't harm humans directly. But by eating all the crops in their path, they can create famines that kill thousands of people.

Before and after a locust swarm arrives

34

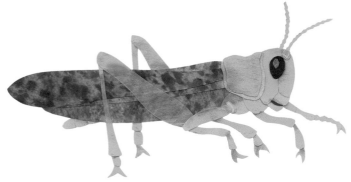

A desert locust in its solitary form

A desert locust after changing into its gregarious (social) form

Locust swarms are also called *locust plagues*. There have been hundreds of these plagues around the world over the course of human history. A swarming locust eats its body weight in food every day.

The desert locust is usually harmless and solitary, but it can become voracious and social. The transition begins when a population of locusts is stressed by drought. If this dry period is followed by lots of rain and new vegetation, the insects change. Their bodies turn yellow, and they begin to produce many more offspring. Soon billions of these insects take to the air, moving in giant swarms.

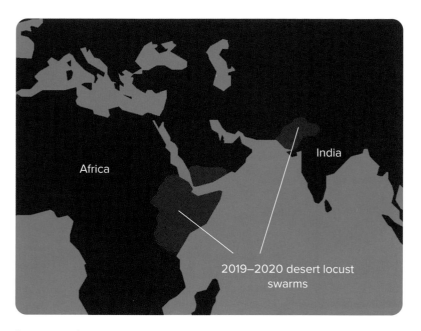

Africa

India

2019–2020 desert locust swarms

A recent plague

In 2019 and 2020, the largest locust swarms seen in 70 years devastated crops in East Africa, the Middle East, India, and Pakistan. In serious plagues, once the locusts have consumed all the vegetation, they eat paper, clothing, and even the wool off sheep.

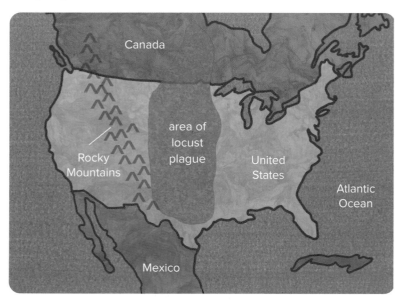

Canada

area of locust plague

Rocky Mountains

United States

Atlantic Ocean

Mexico

An American plague

In 1875, Rocky Mountain locusts swarmed over an area that stretched from Canada to Texas. Trillions of locusts darkened the sky. People reported that the swarm took several days to pass overhead. But by 1902, the Rocky Mountain locust was extinct. It was probably a victim of farmers who were plowing new fields, killing the locusts' underground eggs.

Payback

Locusts are a good source of protein. Many people in Asia and Africa eat them.

The biggest killer

When a serious infectious disease spreads to many countries — or the whole world — in a short period of time, it's called a pandemic. Throughout history, pandemics have killed more people, by far, than any other natural disaster. These diseases are caused by viruses or bacteria, organisms too small to see without a microscope.

Small and smaller

As tiny as bacteria are, viruses are even smaller. They are not alive, but not exactly dead. A virus doesn't do anything until it gets into the cell of a living organism. Then it reproduces by turning the cell into a factory to make thousands of copies of itself, which go on to infect more cells.

About 70 million bubonic plague bacteria could fit in a circle this size.

But 80 billion influenza viruses could fit in the same circle.

Three pandemics

Historians believe that these were three of the deadliest pandemics of the past two thousand years. The pie charts show the estimated percentage (in red) of the world's population that perished in each pandemic.

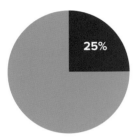

Justinian Plague
541–542
world population:
   200 million
deaths: 50 million

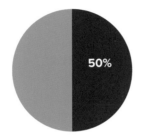

Black Death
1347–1351
world population:
   400 million
deaths: 200 million

influenza pandemic
1918
world population:
   1,800 million
deaths: 50 million

An influenza virus (left) and a bubonic plague bacterium (right) (both enlarged 15,000 times)

Black Death: the worst of them all

Bubonic plague is also known as the Black Death. Bubonic plague pandemics have probably killed more people than any other. There are still a few small outbreaks of the plague today. Fortunately, we can now cure this disease.

Bubonic plague bacteria were transmitted to humans by flea bites. Rats carried the fleas from place to place.

Spread of the plague, 1347–1351

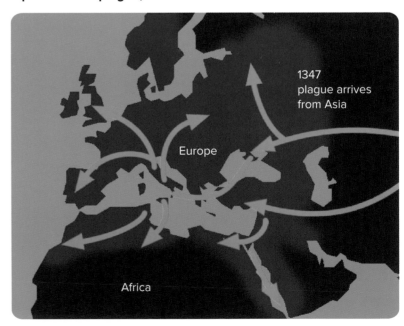

1347 plague arrives from Asia

Europe

Africa

There have been many outbreaks of the plague over the centuries. The worst was in the fourteenth century, when as much as half the world's population died. As many as 200 million people may have perished in this pandemic.

A success story

Smallpox rivals the plague as the deadliest disease in human history. Millions around the world died as repeated smallpox pandemics erupted.

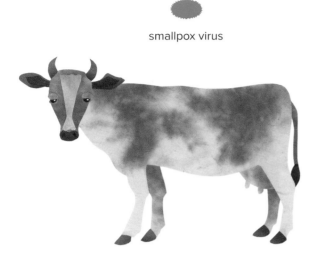

smallpox virus

Smallpox was caused by a virus. Cowpox is a similar but much less deadly disease. In 1796, an English doctor took pus from the sores of a woman with cowpox and inserted it into the arm of a young boy. The child was protected against smallpox — it was the first successful vaccination. In 1980, smallpox was officially declared eradicated. This is considered the world's greatest public health achievement.

A flu pandemic

In 1918, an especially virulent strain of influenza — the flu — spread around the globe. It was the worst pandemic in recent history, killing more than 50 million people.

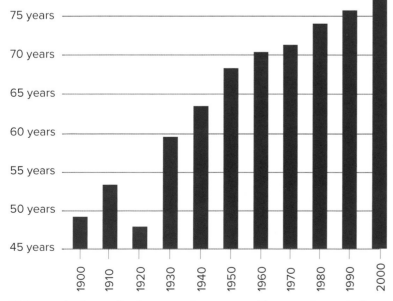

This graph shows the increase in average life expectancy in the United States from 1900 to 2000. There's a big decline just after 1918 due to deaths from the flu pandemic.

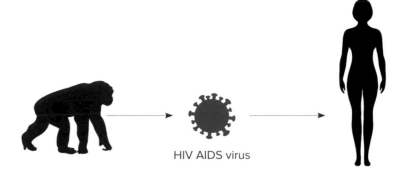

HIV AIDS virus

A modern plague

In the 1980s, HIV AIDS, a disease that had jumped from chimpanzees to people, was recognized by science. Since then, 32 million people around the world have died from AIDS, which damages the body's immune system. AIDS can be controlled with medicine, but hundreds of thousands of people, mostly in underdeveloped countries, die of the disease every year.

A new threat

In China in late 2019, a virus thought to have moved from bats to humans began to make people sick. The virus was similar to others that cause flu, but it was more contagious and more lethal. It causes a disease know as COVID-19. Millions of people around the world have died from the virus.

The virus that causes COVID-19

The virus is spread through tiny droplets coughed, sneezed, or breathed out. Wearing a mask is one of the best ways to protect against spreading or contracting the disease.

Near-Earth Objects

Along with the moons and planets, there are millions of asteroids and perhaps a trillion comets in our solar system. Most of them stay far away from Earth. But more than 22,000 of these objects are larger than 500 feet (152 meters) in diameter, and they have orbits that can bring them uncomfortably close to our planet. They are called NEOs, or Near-Earth Objects.

What is an asteroid?

Asteroids are chunks of rock that orbit the Sun, mostly between the orbits of Mars and Jupiter. They range in diameter from 3½ feet (1 meter) to more than 600 miles (966 kilometers) across.

What is a comet?

Comets have been called "dirty snowballs." They are clumps of rock and ice left over from the formation of the solar system. Most comets are a few miles in diameter.

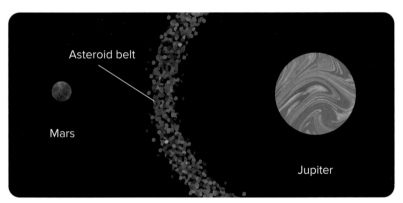

Asteroid belt

Mars

Jupiter

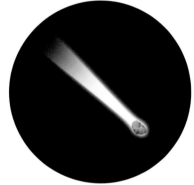

As a comet travels through the solar system, a long tail of dust and gas trails behind, always pointing away from the Sun. About 100 comets have orbits that could make them dangerous to our planet.

How often does a Near-Earth Object collide with us?

Once a year or so an SUV-size asteroid burns up in the atmosphere, causing little damage.

About once every 100 years an asteroid around 100 feet (30 meters) in diameter enters the atmosphere, where it usually burns up or explodes high in the air before hitting the ground. Such an explosion can cause serious local damage.

An asteroid about 300 feet (90 meters) in diameter hits Earth about once every 5,000 years. The impact of an object this size could destroy a large city.

An object larger than about one-half mile (800 meters) in diameter collides with Earth about once every 500,000 years, an event that can cause global devastation and mass extinctions.

 House shown for scale

Impact effects

Asteroids frequently enter Earth's atmosphere. Most are small and break up before they reach the ground, causing little damage. Impacts by larger asteroids or comets are rare, but they can be catastrophic. What happens when one of these big objects collides with our planet? We know because 66 million years ago an asteroid about ten miles (16 kilometers) wide slammed into our planet.

The Tunguska event: the largest impact in recorded history

In 1908, an object about 300 feet (91 meters) across exploded in the air above the Siberian forest. It was as powerful as a large nuclear bomb, and it flattened an estimated 80 million trees. Fortunately, it occurred in an almost uninhabited area, and there were few fatalities.

Reconstructing a 66-million-year-old disaster

The asteroid was moving at ten times the speed of a bullet. It struck what is now the Yucatán Peninsula in Mexico.

Almost instantly, a fireball hotter than the surface of the Sun broiled any living thing within 500 miles (805 kilometers).

A few minutes later a powerful earthquake rocked the entire planet, throwing rocks, trees, and animals into the air.

Soon, red-hot rocks began to rain down. They varied in size from pebbles to giant boulders.

If anything within hundreds of miles survived, it was blown away by a blast of wind moving at the speed of a jet airplane.

A tsunami almost a mile (1,609 meters) high washed over the land. It could have been the tallest wave the world has ever seen.

Some debris from the impact was blasted halfway to the Moon. Meanwhile, the earth had rotated, so the rocks, which got red-hot as they returned to the earth, started fires on the other side of the planet.

Dust and ash blocked the Sun. Months of darkness and cold followed. Perhaps 75 percent of all animal species, including the dinosaurs (except for their close cousins, the birds), were driven to extinction.

Collision course

There is not much chance of a large asteroid or comet striking Earth anytime soon. But when it comes to world-changing impacts, it's a matter of *when,* not *if.* Sooner or later — it could be next week or thousands of years from now — a dangerous object will be headed right for us.

A recent event

In 2013, a meteor about 66 feet (20 meters) wide streaked through the sky above Chelyabinsk, a city in Russia. It disintegrated in the air and exploded with the force of a nuclear bomb. The blast damaged thousands of buildings and injured more than 1,500 people, most by flying glass. Luckily, no one was killed.

An asteroid (or piece of an asteroid or comet) that burns up in Earth's atmosphere is called a *meteor.* If it hits the ground, it is called a *meteorite.*

Estimated size of the 2013 Russian meteor

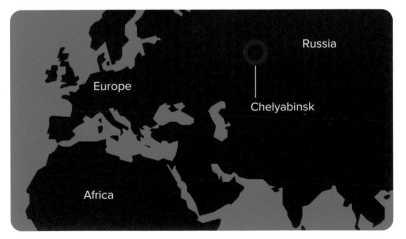

What can we do?

If we find an asteroid that is likely to hit our planet, we will need to change its orbit so that it misses us. Here are a few of the ways we might prevent a collision.

Ram it

One idea is to crash a satellite into the asteroid. If we find the object early enough, we'll only have to nudge it slightly. This will move it into a new orbit that misses us.

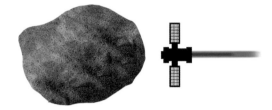

Zap it

Another concept involves firing lasers at the asteroid. The lasers will vaporize some of the rocky surface, creating a force that shoves the object into a different orbit.

Tug it

If we have enough time, parking a heavy spaceship next to the asteroid might work. The gravity of the ship will slowly tug the object onto a different path.

Nuke it

Unlike in the movies, we wouldn't want to blow up the asteroid. This could result in a lot of smaller pieces still headed toward Earth. But a nuclear bomb set off at a greater distance from the asteroid might push it out of a collision course.

Future disasters

Astronomers have witnessed events far from Earth — some of them incredibly violent — that could be disastrous for life on our planet if they were closer. Fortunately, most of them are so distant and infrequent that they are unlikely to affect us for millions or billions of years.

A rogue planet

A rogue planet is one that once orbited a star, but was ejected from its solar system. Perhaps another star passed close by and its gravity kicked the planet out of its orbit. There may be billions of these dark, solitary planets drifting through space. Could one collide with Earth? Luckily, space is so big and empty that there is very little chance of this happening.

Supernova

An aging large star can collapse and explode, briefly outshining its entire galaxy. This explosion is called a supernova. One occurring closer than 30 light years would bombard our planet with enough energy to cause mass extinctions. A supernova occurs this close to us only about once every 240 million years. Astronomers believe that we are safe for now.

Gamma ray burst

A gamma ray burst, or GRB, is a rare and violent release of energy when a large star implodes. These distant events are more powerful than anything we've seen in the universe. If a GRB happens within a few thousand light years of us, the radiation could destroy much of Earth's protective ozone layer and allow harmful radiation from the Sun to reach the surface.

The ultimate disaster

Like all stars, our Sun will die. In about five billion years, it will become a red giant. It will grow so large that it may engulf and vaporize Earth. Long before that happens, the Sun will grow hot enough to boil away the oceans and end life on our planet. But don't worry — that won't happen for another billion years or so.

It's getting hotter

Over millions of years, Earth's temperature has varied. At times, the planet was covered in ice and snow. Other periods have seen higher temperatures — even forests at the South Pole. Now the planet is getting warmer. And it's heating up much more quickly than in the past. Humans are responsible for most of this change. For the past 150 years, we've been burning fossil fuels that add greenhouse gases to the atmosphere.

Greenhouse gas emissions by world region

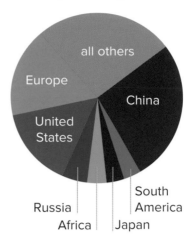

all others
Europe
United States
China
Russia
Africa
Japan
South America

What's the difference between weather and climate?
Weather describes conditions in the atmosphere over a short period of time: How hot, cold, wet, dry, or windy is it? Weather changes from day to day and is different in different places. Climate also changes and varies with location. But climate describes these changes over a period of years, decades, or centuries.

What is the greenhouse effect?

The gases carbon dioxide (CO_2) and methane are produced when we burn coal, oil, and natural gas. They are greenhouse gases, which means they add to the greenhouse effect.

1 Radiation from the Sun heats the land and water.

2 Some of the Sun's heat is radiated back into space.

3 But greenhouse gases act like a blanket, and trap heat in the atmosphere.

Industry and transportation produce the most greenhouse gases.

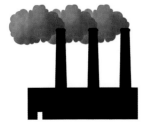

Agriculture and deforestation also add greenhouse gases to the atmosphere. This is because cows belch a surprising amount of methane, and living trees absorb and store carbon dioxide.

Global temperature change and atmospheric carbon dioxide

Carbon dioxide in the atmosphere is measured in parts per million (ppm). This graph show how Earth's temperature has risen over the past 140 years as CO_2 concentrations have increased.

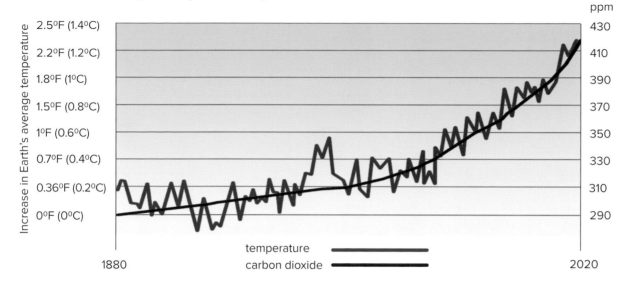

Increase in Earth's average temperature

	ppm
2.5°F (1.4°C)	430
2.2°F (1.2°C)	410
1.8°F (1°C)	390
1.5°F (0.8°C)	370
1°F (0.6°C)	350
0.7°F (0.4°C)	330
0.36°F (0.2°C)	310
0°F (0°C)	290

temperature ——————
carbon dioxide ——————

1880   2020

sea level in 2020
2000
1980
1960
1940
1920
1900
sea level in 1880

Actual sea level rise over the past 140 years (8½ inches • 22 centimeters)

Changes caused by global warming are already showing up.

Changing seasons

In many parts of the world, spring is coming earlier and fall is arriving later.

Melting ice caps

The polar regions are losing ice at a rapid rate. Animals that depend on the ice floes for hunting and safety are becoming endangered.

Spreading tropical diseases

Ticks, mosquitoes, and other organisms that live in warm climates and spread disease are moving into parts of the world that used to be too cold for them.

Vanishing glaciers

All over the world, glaciers are melting or moving faster.

More powerful storms

Warmer ocean water produces stronger hurricanes.

More intense fires

Wildfires are burning hotter and longer as rising temperatures dry out vegetation.

The future

We're just beginning to see the effects of a hotter climate. These effects will become more apparent — and more serious — as time goes on. Climate prediction is complex, and we could experience dramatic, unexpected changes. Much will depend upon how successful the world can be at reducing greenhouse gas emissions.

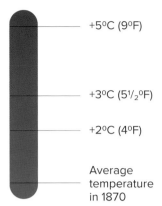

+5°C (9°F)

+3°C (5½°F)

+2°C (4°F)

Average temperature in 1870

How hot will it get?

Our goal is to limit warming to less than 2°C (4°F) above pre-industrial levels by 2100. Many scientists believe a 3°C (5½°F) figure is more likely. And if we continue to burn increasing amounts of fossil fuels, a 5°C (9°F) increase is possible. (*Scientists use degrees Celsius (°C) when referencing global warming, so those units appear first on these pages.*)

The climate change feedback loop

Many of the effects of climate change have a feedback effect, which causes a warming planet to heat up even faster.

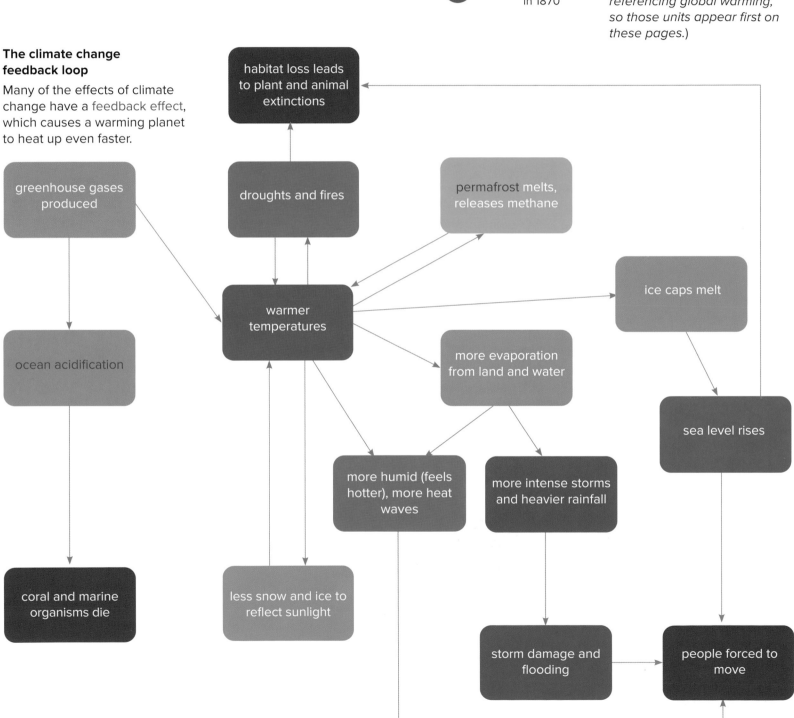

Ice caps

Most of the world's fresh water exists in the form of ice and snow. And 99 percent of that frozen water is held in the ice caps of Greenland and Antarctica. This ice is melting at a rapidly increasing rate. Still, it will take thousands of years for it to disappear completely.

Greenland and Antarctica shown at true relative size

Warmer seas

As the oceans heat up, they absorb more CO_2 and become more acidic. This could result in the death of all the world's coral reefs by 2100.

Greenland

About 9 percent of the world's ice is in Greenland, where the ice cap is 14,000 feet (4,267 meters) deep in some places. If all this ice were to melt, it would raise sea level by 25 feet (8 meters).

Antarctica

The continent at the South Pole holds 90 percent of the world's ice. The oceans would rise about 200 feet (61 meters) if all this ice melted.

Gone forever

One-third to one-half of all plant and animal species could become extinct by 2100. Climate-related effects will be responsible for many of these extinctions.

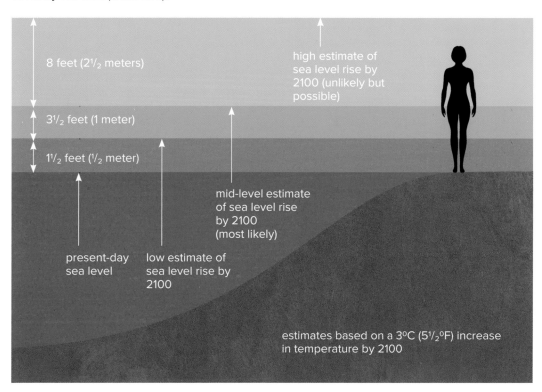

8 feet (2½ meters)

3½ feet (1 meter)

1½ feet (½ meter)

high estimate of sea level rise by 2100 (unlikely but possible)

mid-level estimate of sea level rise by 2100 (most likely)

present-day sea level

low estimate of sea level rise by 2100

estimates based on a 3°C (5½°F) increase in temperature by 2100

The water is rising

One of the most visible effects of a warmer climate is sea level rise. Some of this rise is a result of ocean water expanding as it gets warmer. As time goes on, however, much of it will be from melting ice caps. A 3½ foot (1 meter) rise in sea level would flood many coastal cities around the world and displace millions of people.

Geoengineering

Some scientists are proposing engineering solutions to the problem of climate change. These include spraying reflective substances from jets flying high in the atmosphere or finding ways to capture CO_2 and store it underground.

Do we have time to prevent the most serious effects of climate change?

Even if we stopped burning all fossil fuels now, the climate would continue to warm for decades. We could probably find ways to adjust to that amount of warming. We don't have much time, however, before it will be too late to stop more serious damage to the environment.

anvil
A heavy metal block with a flat surface used for pounding other pieces of metal — which are often heated — into specific shapes (such as a horseshoe).

black hole
An object in space with such density and intense gravity that nothing — not even light — can escape. Most black holes form when large stars collapse violently at the end of their life. Other black holes can be formed when two smaller stars merge.

breached
Broken or ruptured. In the case of a dike, a breach is an opening made so that the water being held back can escape.

catastrophic
Disastrous; often especially deadly or damaging.

core
The hot, dense center of the earth. It has a liquid outer layer and a solid inner sphere made of iron and other metals. The core is more than 2,000 miles (about 3,200 kilometers) in diameter. The movement of liquid iron in the core generates Earth's magnetic field.

debris
The fragments and broken pieces of natural or man-made objects. In a tornado, debris can include rocks, tree limbs, traffic signs, pieces of destroyed buildings, and more.

deforestation
The loss of all the trees in an area through natural causes, such as fire or drought, or by logging or other human activity.

depleted
Decreased supply; used up.

devastating
Disastrous; especially destructive.

dikes
Built-up soil, sand, or other material used to hold back the waters of a river, lake, or sea.

disorientation
Confusion, loss of a sense of direction or purpose.

eradicate
To completely get rid of something. Eradication can be local (killing all the cockroaches in a building) or global (as in the worldwide elimination of the smallpox virus).

extinction
The loss of all the members of a living species, or the death of an entire group of organisms.

feedback effect
When the output of a system or process is fed back into the same process. The feedback effect can magnify the consequences of a process.

fossil fuels
Fuels derived from the remains of ancient living things. Coal, oil, and natural gas are all fossil fuels. They were largely created by dead plants that accumulated over millions of years. This plant material was buried by layers of soil and rock, and heat and pressure converted the organic material to fuel.

gregarious
Sociable. In animals, living in groups, herds, or flocks.

groundwater
Water found in the spaces between underground particles of soil and rock.

humidity
A measure of the amount of water vapor in the air. Warm air holds more moisture than cold air. Humidity is measured as a percentage of the amount of water vapor that can exist in the air at a given temperature. One hundred percent humidity means that the air can contain no more moisture.

immune system
A network of cells and systems in the body that fight disease-causing organisms.

implode
To collapse violently. A large star implodes to become a black hole.

lethal
Deadly or fatal.

light year
The distance light travels in one year. Light moves at 186,000 miles per second (300,000 kilometers per second). In a year, light will travel almost six trillion miles ($9\frac{1}{2}$ trillion kilometers).

magnetic field
An invisible field around a magnet that affects electrical currents and charged particles, such as those coming from the Sun.

mantle
A layer of solid and partially molten rock approximately 1,800 miles (about 2,900 kilometers) thick. It lies between Earth's rocky crust and its solid core.

mass extinction
An event that kills three-quarters or more of Earth's living species. There have been at least five mass extinctions over the past few hundred million years. We are currently in the sixth mass extinction. This sixth extinction is due to habitat loss and climate change caused by humans.

nausea
An uneasy feeling in the stomach that may lead to throwing up.

Northern Hemisphere
The part of the globe north of the equator.

ocean acidification
Carbon dioxide gas in the atmosphere dissolves in ocean water and makes carbonic acid, which is harmful to living things in the sea.

orbit
A circular or elliptical path followed by an object as it rotates around another object, such as the Moon's path around the earth.

permafrost
Soil found in the polar regions and at high altitudes that remains frozen year-round. Large areas of permafrost are thawing as the climate warms, with potentially serious consequences that we don't fully understand.

phenomenon
An observed event that is often unusual or impressive.

plummet
To plunge or fall suddenly.

pre-industrial
A time before the industrial revolution (which began in the late 1700s) and before the widespread use of heavy machinery and fossil fuels.

retardant
A substance that slows or stops an event or process, such as a fire.

saturated
Completely filled; unable to hold more (e.g., a sponge can be saturated with water).

Siberia
A vast region of northern Russia. It is extremely cold in the winter, and mostly covered in a dense evergreen forest.

suffocation
Death caused by lack of oxygen or the ability to breathe.

sulphuric acid
A chemical compound. When concentrated, it is a clear, oily liquid. It is highly corrosive to metal, flesh, and other organic material.

tectonic plates
The solid outer layer of our planet is broken into seven large plates and more than a dozen smaller ones. They vary in thickness from 10 miles (16 kilometers) to 125 miles (201 kilometers). These plates — and the landmasses on them — drift slowly, gradually changing the shape and position of the continents.

turbulent
Jumbled and chaotic, moving rapidly in a disorderly way.

updraft
An upward movement of air. Hot air is lighter than cold air. In a fire, heated air rises, creating an updraft.

vaccination
The introduction, often by injection, of small amounts of a disease-causing virus or bacteria into a human or animal. These dangerous organisms are killed or made less virulent before being used in a vaccine. The vaccine causes the recipient's body to create antibodies to the disease — cells that will attack the dangerous form of the virus or bacteria if it is encountered.

virulent
Extremely toxic or harmful.

voracious
Having a huge appetite, eating rapidly and excessively.

vulnerable
Susceptible to harm or damage.

Bibliography

100 Most Destructive Natural Disasters. By Anna Claybourne. Scholastic, 2014.

Around the World: The Atlas for Today. Edited by Andrew Losowsky, Sven Ehmann, and Robert Klanten. Gestalten, 2013.

The Complete Guide to Extreme Weather. By Louise Spilsbury and Anna Claybourne. Sandy Creek, 2016.

The Dynamics of Disaster. By Susan W. Kieffer. W. W. Norton and Company, 2013.

Earth by the Numbers. By Steve Jenkins. Houghton Mifflin Harcourt, 2019.

Earth Explained. By Barbara Taylor. A Henry Holt Reference Book, 1997.

Earth-Shattering Events. By Robin Jacobs. Cicada Books, 2020.

Incredible Earth. By Nick Clifford. DK Publishing, 1996.

My Best Book of Volcanoes. By Simon Adams. Kingfisher, 2001.

Natural Disasters. By Dougal Dixon. The Reader's Digest Association Limited, 1997.

Superstats: Extreme Planet. By Moira Butterfield. Little Bee Books, 2015.

Volcano & Earthquake. By Susanna Van Rose. DK Eyewitness Books, 2014.

For Jeffrey

All rights reserved. For information about permission to reproduce
selections from this book, write to trade.permissions@hmhco.com
or to Permissions, Houghton Mifflin Harcourt Publishing Company,
3 Park Avenue, 19th Floor, New York, New York 10016.

hmhbooks.com

The illustrations are cut- and torn-paper collage.
The infographics are cut-paper silhouettes and graphics created digitally.
The text type was set in Proxima Nova.
The display type was set in Base Nine.

ISBN: 978-1-328-56948-6

Manufactured in Hong Kong
1010P 10 9 8 7 6 5 4 3 2 1
4500826878